Thanksgiving

by **Trudi Strain Trueit**

Reading Consultant: Nanci R. Vargus, Ed.D.

Marshall Cavendish
Benchmark
New York

Picture Words

 books

 dogs

 family

 hands

 mittens

pumpkin pie

 school

 toys

 turkey

We hold 🙌 and give thanks.

I am thankful for .

I am thankful for .

I am thankful for .

I am thankful for 🧤.

I am thankful for .

I am thankful for .

I am thankful for .

I am thankful for .
Happy Thanksgiving!

Words to Know

family (FAM-uh-lee)
   a group of people who share
   the same relatives

thankful (THANK-fuhl)
   feeling or showing thanks

Thanksgiving (thanks-GIV-ing)
   a U.S. holiday on the fourth
   Thursday of November celebrated
   with big dinners and giving thanks

Find Out More

Books

Kroll, Virginia L. *The Thanksgiving Bowl*. Gretna, LA : Pelican, 2007.

Mercer, Abbie. *Happy Thanksgiving*. New York: PowerKids Press, 2008.

Prelutsky, Jack. *It's Thanksgiving!* New York: HarperCollins, 2008.

Websites

Pilgrim Hall Museum
www.pilgrimhall.org/thanksg.htm

Plimoth Plantation
www.plimoth.org/kids

The Smithsonian Institution: Thanksgiving in America
www.si.edu/Encyclopedia_SI/nmah/thanks.htm

About the Author

Trudi Strain Trueit is thankful for her home in the Pacific Northwest and her husband, Bill. She is the author of more than fifty fiction and nonfiction books for children, including *Christmas* and *Hanukkah* in the Benchmark Rebus Holiday Fun series. Visit her website at **www.truditrueit.com**.

About the Reading Consultant

Nanci R. Vargus, Ed.D., wants all children to enjoy reading. She used to teach first grade. Now she works at the University of Indianapolis. Nanci helps young people become teachers. She enjoys celebrating Thanksgiving with all her grandchildren—Charlotte, Corinne, Adara Joy, Oliver, and Christopher.

Copyright © 2011 Marshall Cavendish Corporation

Published by Marshall Cavendish Benchmark
An imprint of Marshall Cavendish Corporation

Website: www.marshallcavendish.us

This publication represents the opinions and views of the author based on Trudi Strain Trueit's personal experience, knowledge, and research. The information in this book serves as a general guide only. The author and publisher have used their best efforts in preparing this book and disclaim liability rising directly and indirectly from the use and application of this book.

Other Marshall Cavendish Offices:
Marshall Cavendish International (Asia) Private Limited, 1 New Industrial Road, Singapore 536196 • Marshall Cavendish International (Thailand) Co Ltd. 253 Asoke, 12th Flr, Sukhumvit 21 Road, Klongtoey Nua, Wattana, Bangkok 10110, Thailand • Marshall Cavendish (Malaysia) Sdn Bhd, Times Subang, Lot 46, Subang Hi-Tech Industrial Park, Batu Tiga, 40000 Shah Alam, Selangor Darul Ehsan, Malaysia

Marshall Cavendish is a trademark of Times Publishing Limited

All websites were available and accurate when this book was sent to press.

Library of Congress Cataloging-In-Publication Data
Trueit, Trudi Strain.
Thanksgiving / Trudi Strain Trueit.
        p. cm. — (Benchmark rebus. Holiday fun)
Includes bibliographical references.
Summary: "A simple introduction to Thanksgiving using rebuses"—Provided by publisher.
ISBN 978-0-7614-4888-4
1. Thanksgiving Day—Juvenile literature. 2. Rebuses—Juvenile literature. I. Title.
GT4975.T78 2010
2009019099

Editor: Christina Gardeski
Publisher: Michelle Bisson
Art Director: Anahid Hamparian
Series Designer: Virginia Pope

Photo research by Connie Gardner
Cover photo by Ron Nickel/*Art Life Images*

The photographs in this book are used by permission and through the courtesy of:
Corbis: p. 5 Arthur Klonsky; p. 7 LWA Sharie Kennedy; p. 9 Jim Craigmyle; p. 11 John Francis Bourke. *Art Life Images*: p. 13 Banana Stock; p. 21 Comstock. *Alamy*: p. 15 Norbert Shaefer; p. 19 Ryan McVay. *Getty Images*: p. 2 art parner-images, books; Sharon Montrose, dogs; Jose Luis Pelaez, family; Last Resort, hands; Seide Preis, mittens; p. 3 Acme Food arts, pumpkin pie; Dave King, toys; ThinkStock, turkey; p. 17 stockbyte. *Super Stock*: p. 3 age fotostock, school.

Printed in Malaysia (T)
1 3 5 6 4 2